Night-

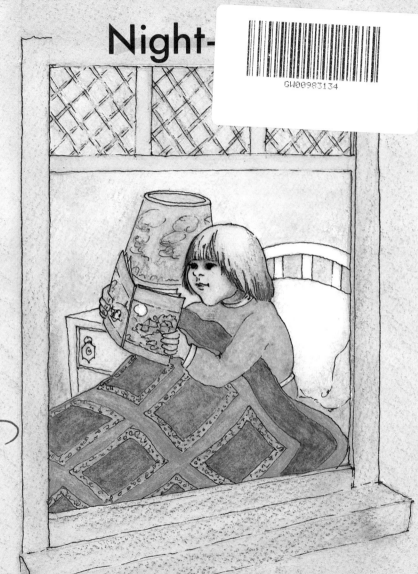

Lovely 1.61R

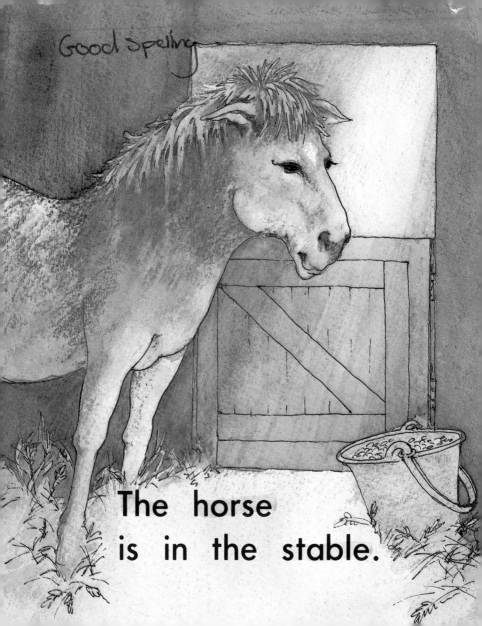

The horse
is in the stable.

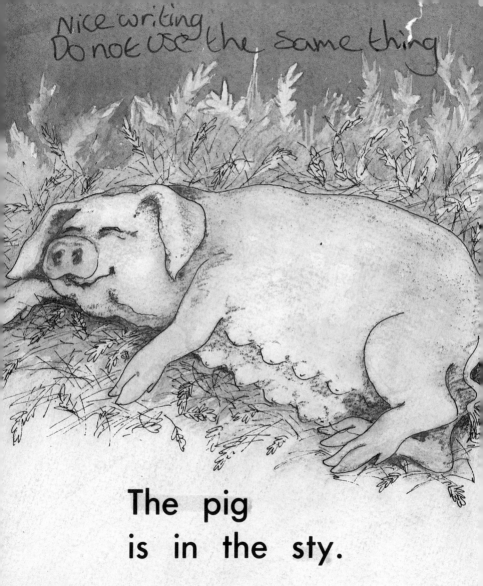

The pig
is in the sty.

3

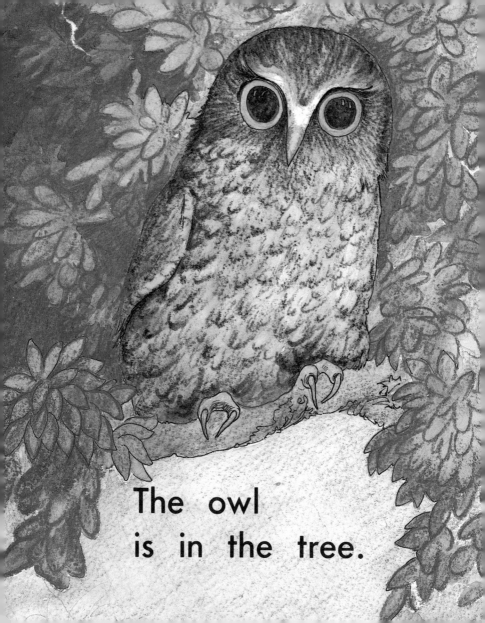

The owl
is in the tree.

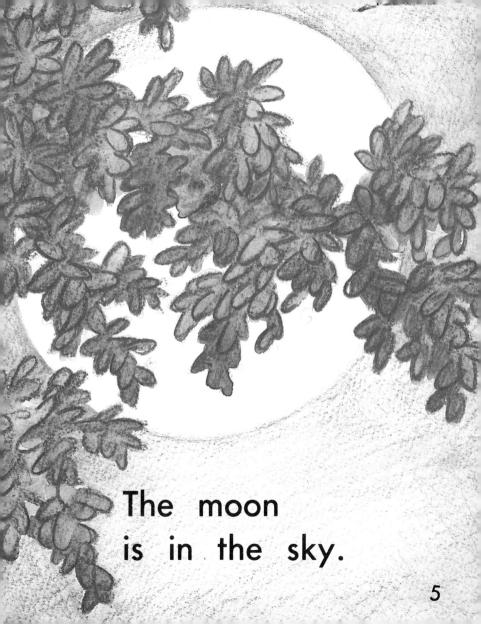

The moon
is in the sky.

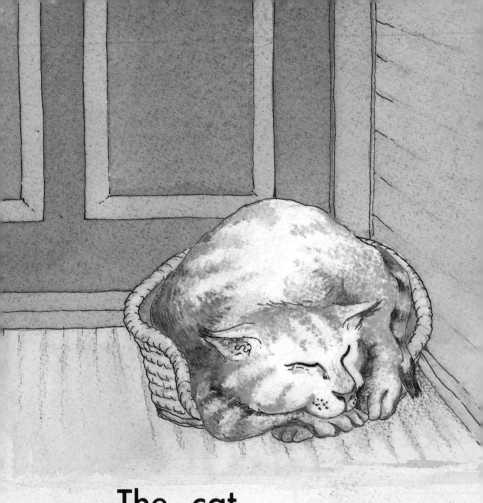

The cat
is in the basket.

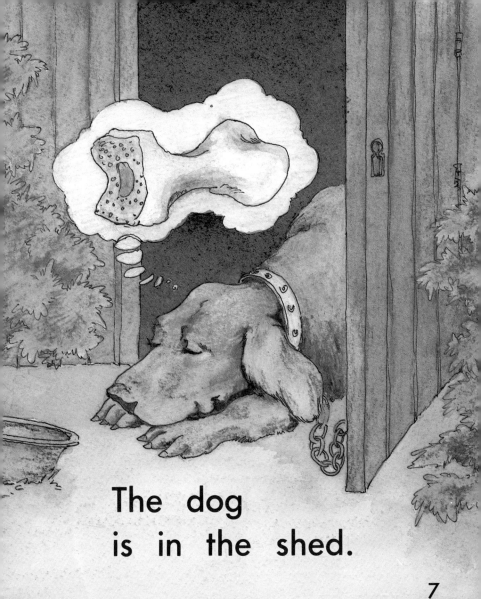

The dog
is in the shed.

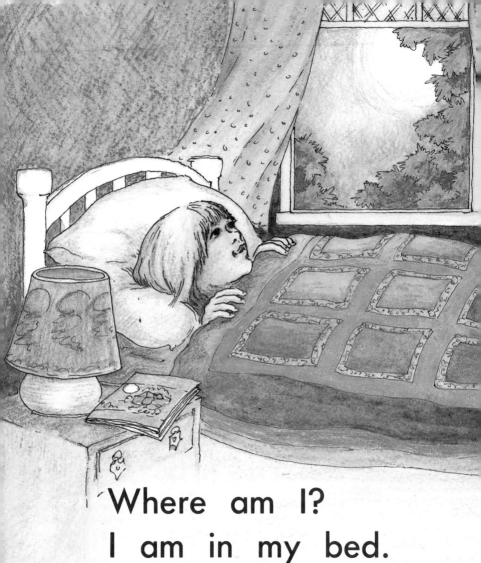

Where am I?
I am in my bed.